Basic Skill

Reading Comprehension

Grade 6

Table of Contents

Frank Schaffer Publications®

Instructional Fair is an imprint of Frank Schaffer Publications.

Printed in the United States of America. All rights reserved.
Limited Reproduction Permission: Permission to duplicate
these materials is limited to the person for whom they are purchased. Reproduction for an entire school or school district
is unlawful and strictly prohibited. Frank Schaffer Publications
is an imprint of School Specialty Publishing.
Copyright © 1996 School Specialty Publishing.

ISBN 1-56822-252-1

4 5 6 7 8 9 10 PAT 10 09 08

Author: Norm Sneller
Editors: Elizabeth Flikkema, Sharon
Kirkwood, Kathleen Vaughn
Cover Artist: Cindy Cutler
Interior Designer: Pat Geasler
Interior Artist: Don O'Connor

Send all inquiries to:
Frank Schaffer Publications
8720 Orion Place
Columbus, OH 43240-2111

Name _____

Accidents Do Happen

On Wednesday, Sean D. Keene was worried. Two weeks earlier, Mr. Tuit, the physical science teacher, had assigned Sean's class a realism assignment: Describe an occurrence of force and motion in everyday terms. The assignment was due Thursday. Sean had not begun.

Because Sean had missed last week's classes due to chicken pox, he didn't have a clue as to what force and motion were. When Sean heard the word "force," he thought of those ancient Star Wars movies; when he heard the word "motion," he imagined car sickness.

Dashing home from school, Sean immediately sat down to plan his attack. Distracted by his hunger, he sauntered off to the bulk-food bin in the pantry, grabbed a half-dozen walnuts, and cracked them open with his grandma's antique nutcracker. Ouch! Sean accidentally squeezed the machine on his pinky. Pain darted through his hand and arm.

Sean dropped the walnuts just as he heard his dad returning from work. Dad reminded Sean of his promise to tear out the old tree fort. The fort, a remnant of Sean's creative but disorganized past, was a dilapidated structure of rusty nails, rotting wood, and mangled rope situated on three branches overhanging the family's paved driveway.

Holding a crowbar in his hand, Sean gingerly climbed an extension ladder to gain access to the fort. He pried out nail after nail, dropping hunks of the rotting fort to the pavement below. "I sure love destroying stuff," he thought to himself. Just then Sean pried out a spike with a bit too much vigor. The nail shot out of its wooden prison. The crowbar tip snapped back, catching Sean

across the corner of his forehead.

Ten minutes later, with the flow of blood from his noggin stemmed, his worrisome dad felt reassured that x-rays were unneeded. Sean staggered back outside, broom in hand, to clean up the debris on the driveway. With every half-dozen swipes of the broom, Sean bent over to gather the junk into an over-sized dustpan and emptied it into a trash barrel.

Sean was tired and angry. His pinky throbbed and his head was spinning. He had no time for this! Shouldn't school come first? With righteous indignation, Sean took a mighty swipe and ... crack! ... the broom fractured the radius bone of his left arm.

The following afternoon each student shared a realism report for science. When Sean's turn came, he stood up. No paper in hand—he was in the emergency room half the night—Sean detailed his sorry excuse. He spoke clearly, dramatically, even emotionally. He described the nutcracker, the crowbar, and the broom. Then, looking down at his wristwatch which read 2:13, Sean muttered "Two-one-three."

"Exactly!" chortled Mr. Tuit who was perched on his desk. "Using everyday terms, you have just described force and motion with simple machine levers 2, 1, and 3. Class, please join me in honoring this budding scientist."

Name _____

Accidents Do Happen

Main Character: _____

Setting: _____

Problem: _____

_____

_____

_____

Key Events:

1. _____

_____

2. _____

_____

3. _____

_____

4. _____

_____

5. _____

_____

Solution to problem:

_____

_____

Evaluation:

_____

_____

Extension: Draw pictures to illustrate the 3 lever types. Use words such as fulcrum, force, and load. List examples of each from the story.

Name _____

Mow-'Em-Down

Francesca Fontaine was in seventh heaven. Her English teacher, Mrs. Candy Gramme, gave Francesca permission to write a biographical sketch on her favorite sport star. Francesca's "fave" was the totally-hot Matt "Mow-'Em-Down" Mulroney of the Bismarck Moles. Here is her report:

My report is about Matt Mulroney, the greatest defensive lineman who ever played football. Matt was born to Mule and Madeleine Mulroney thirty-two years ago in Onion Falls. He was born with smoky brown eyes—just like his dad's. Matt was adored by his two younger brothers, Chuckie and Wayne, and by Rasputin, the family collie. While in middle school, Matt earned top grades in advanced algebra and life science. In high school, he chipped off part of a tooth during a scrimmage. This resulted in Matt's ability to whistle team plays in a special code that only his teammates recognized. Always in excellent health, Matt grew to 6 feet 4 inches tall. By the age of 23, Matt reached his optimum playing weight of 297 pounds.

During college, Matt worked hard to earn extra money. He worked for the Guernsey Dairy Conglomerate 20 hours a week to make ends meet. One day while walking home from work, Matt witnessed a bank robbery. He intercepted the get-away vehicle—a red Toyota pickup truck. He grabbed hold of the tailgate so the thieves could not move forward. Fortunately, the pickup was not able to shift into reverse. When police arrived and apprehended the two criminals, one of the suspects muttered, "I wish we had mowed 'em down." And the name stuck.

Matt works out regularly "pumping iron." Every week he puts in 30 hours of strenuous physical training. John Ritum of the Chicago Evening Post calls him "The Ripple" because of the wave-like movement of his muscles. With his long, black hair and size 12 shoes, Matt "Mow-'Em-Down" Mulroney is a most impressive sight.

Two years ago Matt was sidelined for a week. The injury happened when the Winston Smokies had the Moles' defense fooled on an option play; well, all but Matt. He plowed through five of his opponents, leaving them flat on their backs as he stripped the ball from Spud Tato, the tailback, and dove on the pigskin. When the rest of the Smokies were pried off, Matt remained flat on the field.

Matt "Mow-'Em-Down" Mulroney is still my hero. He has appeared on The Tonight Show four times. He is married and has two little girls. Matt makes megabucks but he hasn't forgotten his roots. He comes back to Onion Falls every winter during the off-season.

Name _____

Mow-'Em-Down

Mrs. Gramme was so pleased with Francesca's report that she made copies of the report along with a list of questions to be answered by the entire class. See if you can answer these questions too.

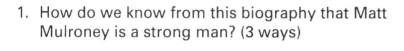

1. How do we know from this biography that Matt Mulroney is a strong man? (3 ways)

   _____

   _____

   _____

2. List three phrases that describe Mr. Mulroney's visual appearance.

   _____

   _____

   _____

3. In what way has Mow-'Em-Down been lucky?

   _____

   _____

4. Tell what position Matt played on the team.

   _____

5. Underline the adjectives that best describe Matt Mulroney.

brave	popular	fearful
vicious	handsome	hard-working
short	blond	muscular
intelligent	sickly	fortunate

Name _____

A Royal Pain

For the unit on European Studies, Kyesha concentrated on England. She was impressed by its royalty. Since she was particularly fascinated with England's early history, she prepared her class speech on King Richard I. Here it is:

Most Americans know England's King Richard as the man who thanked Robin Hood for defending the cause of the poor against greedy noblemen. Richard's brother John and the Sheriff of Nottingham were corrupt enemies of the King. We don't really know if Robin Hood ever met with King Richard even though they lived in the same century. What I learned about King Richard I may shock you.

King Richard, 1157–1199, was a less than honorable king. I will give you four reasons to support this statement.

First, Richard never really grew up. Stories suggest that he fought with his father, the previous king, and his brothers much of his life. He was selfish and even petulant when he did not get his way. Perhaps brother John was a better ruler than Richard, who couldn't sit still for long.

That brings me to my second point. Richard ruled poorly. During the ten years of his reign, he spent only about six months in England. The rest of the time he was in the Holy Land fighting in the Crusades. If one of our presidents tried that, we'd impeach the rascal. Richard left the care of England in the hands of his underlings.

Thirdly, Richard cost England a fortune. Because his wars were so expensive, the English royal treasury was in shambles. On his return from the Crusades, Richard was captured by an Austrian duke who held him

prisoner for the emperor of the Holy Roman Empire. Richard was held captive until England promised to pay a huge ransom. It's a wonder England was willing to dish out the money.

Finally, Richard I lost English-held land to France. Before the Crusade, Richard was king over vast land holdings on the continent. During Richard's imprisonment, Phillip II of France seized some of the land from England. Richard spent the last five years of his reign trying to regain the land.

Name _____

A Royal Pain

Write the central statement of the report in the center of the web. Then list four supporting statements. Finally, give the details that clarify each supporting statement.

Supporting Statement:

_____

_____

|

Details

_____

_____

_____

Supporting Statement:

_____

_____

|

Details

_____

_____

_____

Central Statement

_____

_____

_____

Supporting Statement:

_____

_____

|

Details

_____

_____

_____

Supporting Statement:

_____

_____

|

Details

_____

_____

_____

Extension: Research the Crusades. Find out why they were fought; who fought them; and what the results were.

Metropolis

Miss Sabrina Sivix, a sixth grade social studies instructor, has just presented to her class a unit called *Megalopolis: Chief Cities of the 20th Century.* One of her students, Betsy Moss, frantically took notes on the information Miss Sivix found in Grolier's Encyclopedia. Here are the notes taken by Betsy.

London has a population of 9,115,000.

Buenos Aires is City #10 in population order.

Mexico City has the second greatest population.

Karachi has fewer people than Paris.

Jakarta's population figure is made up of the following digits: 8,0,2,0,9,0,8. The order is from greatest to least.

Paris has 58,000 people less than Delhi which has 337,000 less than London, City #17.

10,156,000 is the population of Manila.

#16 has 9,779,000 people.

The third largest city has a population of 18,701,000.

The Osaka-Kobe-Kyoto megalopolis has a population of 13,872,000.

The three largest population centers have 27,245,000, 20,899,000, and 18,701,000 people, respectively.

The city following Osaka-Kobe-Kyoto has a population of 12,109,000.

Tokyo-Yokohama has a population equal to three times the population of London, minus 100,000 people.

Los Angeles' population of 10,130,000 is 4,495,000 less than New York's.

Cairo's population of 10,099,000 places it in the 14th spot.

The eighth city has a population of 11,898,000.

Jakarta is City #15.

Moscow's population is 10,446,000.

The 20th city has 8,014,000 people.

Tehran immediately follows Jakarta.

Manila, City #12, has 26,000 more people than Los Angeles.

India's cities of Bombay and Calcutta are 7th and 8th, respectively.

São Paulo is the third largest city.

Rio de Janeiro's population of 11,688,000 has just 31,000 more people than #10.

Seoul has 16,792,000 people.

Metropolis

Betsy made less of a muddle with her notes when she completed the following chart. Use the clues from page 8 to organize the city information according to size.

Order of Cities and Their Populations

Order	City	Population
1	_____	_____
2	_____	_____
3	_____	_____
4	_____	_____
5	_____	_____
6	_____	_____
7	_____	_____
8	_____	_____
9	_____	_____
10	_____	_____
11	_____	_____
12	_____	_____
13	_____	_____
14	_____	_____
15	_____	_____
16	_____	_____
17	_____	_____
18	_____	_____
19	_____	_____
20	_____	_____

Extension: Match each of the following countries with the above cities: India (3 cities), Pakistan, the Philippines, Indonesia, Japan (2), South Korea, Iran, Egypt, Russia, France, United Kingdom, Brazil (2), Argentina, Mexico, and the United States (2). Make a chart on the back of this paper.

Name _____

A Special Attraction

When shy and solemn Shanda Lira first arrived at school, she discovered to her absolute horror, that a freckle-faced boy in her sixth-grade class was smitten with her. Because she had just moved into the city from the country, Shanda had not yet made friends with the other kids in her grade. She didn't feel comfortable asking the other students this boy's name. And he certainly didn't offer his name; just a handful of flowers...but they were pretty.

Shanda soon learned the red-haired boy's name was Tommy. He didn't give her flowers anymore, but he did smile his crooked smile in her direction when the class would line up for assembly or gym. Shanda still felt some-what uncomfortable about the attention he gave her, small though it was. What was his attraction to her anyway? He'd never tell her! Shanda tried on several occasions to start a conversation with him, but he'd merely blush, put his hands in his pockets, and look down in embarrassment.

Gradually, Shanda developed a large circle of friends. A couple of really boisterous boys bothered her constantly. Francesca confided that Bob had a crush on her. What a silly word thought Shanda. Crush. Like Bob would smash his face up against a window pane looking at her? He pestered her daily at lunch time, begging for her chips or cookies. Sean was a bit of a pest too, but he knew how to crack people up with his antics. He was always tripping over his shoestrings or pinching his hand in a door or window.

One day as she was walking down the hallway, Tom came up alongside her. "Do you like animals?" He spoke four words!

Shanda turned to him and replied, "Oh, hi, Tommy. I sure do. We have pets at home.

How about you?" Shanda noticed how nervous Tom became as she rambled on. He even appeared to stop breathing. He whispered something about a dog and walked away. Oh! thought Shanda. Did I hurt his feelings when I called him Tommy?

A week later Tom reverently handed Shanda a photo. It was a snapshot taken of a beautiful young collie. She had intelligent eyes and a long nose. Her ears were alert, and her face tilted questioningly. Shanda knew this was an important moment for Tom. "What's her name?" she asked softly.

"Sh, sh, she was Shanda...like you. We had had her since I was in kindergarten; Sh, sh, she's gone now."

Name _____

A Special Attraction

Answer these questions.

1. Why might Tom be attracted to Shanda? Give two plausible explanations.

   _____

   _____

   _____

   _____

2. What might cause Tom to be shy or withdrawn? Give three plausible explanations.

   _____

   _____

   _____

   _____

3. How does Shanda show a caring nature?

   _____

   _____

   _____

4. Imagine that the conversation at the end of the story continues.
   How might you complete it?

   _____

   _____

   _____

   _____

   _____

   _____

   _____

   _____

Extension: Why do you think some people are more affectionate toward animals than others?

Name _____

They're All As

Henry Wadsworth Wordsmith believes he is the smartest person in the sixth grade. That's because he reads his college-level dictionary 45 minutes every evening. Last week he focused on a few of his favorite *A words* as he retold a familiar folk tale.

Here is my abridged and slightly altered form of "The Three Pigs."

One day, a mother agouti abruptly adjourned her unusually large litter of three offspring. She wished to assist them in maturation. Obviously this caused much anguish, but as the adage goes: "No pain, no gain."

The three agoutis left their mother's archaic surroundings which abutted a deep, dark forest. They planned to affiliate with each other in their adventure of post-maternal freedom. However, a cunning hardware salesman suggested that the three were apt to quarrel over their differences. He alluded to their need for utter independence.

The aggregate effect of his suggestion alarmed the agoutis so much that they did indeed part company.

The first agouti built his home of adobe. He set a candle aglow in his front window.

The second followed his agenda and built his home in a manner akin to his first brother.

The third agouti disliked the alienation from his brothers, but eventually he constructed a snug arbor in the aerial reaches of an oak tree.

An amicable dachshund named Dave passed by and called out in adulation of the third agouti's abode.

Imagining affront and treachery the agouti

gave an acerbic response. He called Dave a "mangy critter!"

Of course, no beast worth his mettle will take such abuse. Dave could not tolerate such behavior which gnawed at his craw like an abscess in his paw. He contacted his avuncular relative, an aimless, wandering mutt named Walter. Together they altered the agouti's abhorrent manners.

Name _____

They're All As

Write the letter of the correct meaning on the line to match each of the words from the story.

____agouti   a. disgusting

____abhorrent   b. without purpose

____amicable   c. rodent

____anguish   d. clay

____adjourned   e. friendly

____acerbic   f. distress

____aimless   g. harsh

____adobe   h. dismissed

____arbor   a. like an uncle

____avuncular   b. similar

____adulation   c. frightened

____alarmed   d. isolation

____assist   e. changed

____alienation   f. praise

____akin   g. shady place

____altered   h. help

____abruptly   a. compressed

____alluded   b. insult

____abridged   c. lofty

____affront   d. undertaking

____agenda   e. hinted

____adventure   f. unite

____affiliate   g. without warning

____aerial   h. plan

____apt   a. bordered

____abutted   b. sore

____adage   c. likely

____archaic   d. saying

____aggregate   e. old

____abode   f. total

____abscess   g. dwelling

Kids Say the Darndest Things

Mr. Tuit loves watching and listening to students' responses to life experiences. For three weeks he scribbled notes and taped snippets of conversations. Here are some of the quotes he gathered.

On receiving a heavy load of homework:

A1 "Maybe it's not as bad as it seems. I'm glad it's only ten pages."

A2 "We have homework? Are you sure that's what he said?"

A3 "It makes me sick to my stomach. There! You happy?"

A4 "I'll never get it done. I already have my paper route and basketball practice."

On dissecting earthworms in class:

B1 "No way, no how, never!"

B2 "Oh, the poor thing! Do you think it suffered at all when I cut it?"

B3 "Let me at 'em!"

B4 "Go ahead. You can make the first incision."

On losing a ball game:

C1 "I can't believe I missed the tag!"

C2 "Does this mean we have an extra practice this week?"

C3 "Right now, I just don't care. I'm going home."

C4 "The ump was blind! He needs trifocals or something."

On having a special assembly:

D1 "What! You mean we have to miss math?"

D2 "This is the seventh time we've had Officer Jolly come. Give me a break."

D3 "Did you hear the drummer? He was awesome."

D4 "Oh, I love assemblies. They make me want to sing like a bird."

On opening one's sack lunch:

E1 "Doesn't Mom love me any more?"

E2 "What! This isn't my oatmeal cookie."

E3 "Ah! My favorite. . .apple pie."

E4 "Rats! I was hoping for pretzels."

After organizing the responses, Mr. Tuit posted a copy outside his classroom to observe the reactions of the students when they read them. Some chuckled; others moaned. One girl chortled, "Oh, that one sounds just like my mother!" Wailed another, "I didn't mean it, I really didn't." Mr. Tuit smiled and said, "Kids say the darndest things."

Kids Say the Darndest Things

Match quotes from the previous page with the emotions they project. Use each quote only once.

On receiving homework...

worried _____   disgusted _____

hopeful _____   bewildered _____

On dissecting earthworms...

enthusiastic _____   adamant _____

sympathetic _____   generous _____

On losing a ball game...

embarrassed_____   angry _____

fearful _____   tired _____

On having a special assembly...

joking _____   excited _____

awed _____   bored _____

On opening one's lunch...

surprised _____   satisfied _____

disappointed _____   doubtful _____

Extension: Choose one of the themes from the reading selection. Decide the emotions you would like to project. Write a dialogue to convey those feelings. You may use part of the quotes shown, but you must expand to create a full converstion.

Name _____

Wherefore Art Thou?

Madeline loves to play detective. She loves exploring, searching for clues, and unraveling mysteries. Most of her classmates tolerate her behavior.

One morning, Mrs. Candy Gramme, the English teacher, introduced Shakespeare to Madeline's class. She had removed her earrings to demonstrate medieval helmet gear. During her presentation she noticed that one of her earrings was missing. She could not have removed them more than five minutes earlier. Now, helmet off and hair a'frazzle, Mrs. Gramme was bewildered.

She asked the class to read Act Three, Scene One, while she searched for her jewelry. Mrs. Gramme peered intently around her desk kneeling on all fours. Madeline, never one to sit still very long, quietly rose from her seat in the rear of the room and stealthily snuck toward the front. As she passed Sean, she accidentally stepped on his toe. Sean squelched a scream as he woke from his mid-morning nap.

"What are you doing?" he croaked in his typically raspy whisper.

"If you get me in trouble, I'll squeeze your pinky," Madeline threatened.

Sean immediately stilled.

Madeline stood quietly behind her teacher whose back was to the class. Madeline leaned over, glancing left and right in synchronized movement with Mrs. Gramme, searching for the red polka-dot Minnie Mouse earring. Wait! What was that under the desk?

"There it is!" Madeline shouted. Mrs. Gramme was so startled at the sound of Madeline's voice that she jumped up and fell back into Rosemary Ann Thyme's desk.

Rosemary, who had been leaning back in her chair, fell over, sending her copy of Hamlet sailing to the tiled floor. It exploded into single sheets of Shakespeare, scattering in outrageous fortune.

Madeline was still pointing under Mrs. Gramme's desk. Yes indeed, a mouse-shape was there, but it was hardly an earring. As the sheets of paper were settling, a mouse, holding a red-and-white polka-dot candy wrapper, scampered into the primitive radiator system.

"Oh," said Madeline disappointedly. "Wrong mouse."

"Madeline," said Mrs. Gramme with remarkable patience, "would you rather be a student or a permanent fixture in the principal's office?"

"To be, or not to be: that is the question," pondered Madeline.

Name _____

Wherefore Art Thou?

Madeline caused a chain reaction of unfortunate events. Complete the cause and the effect statement pairs below.

Cause	**Effect**
1. _____ _____	Mrs. Gramme removed her earrings.
2. _____ _____	Mrs. Gramme asked the class to read quietly.
3. Madeline stepped on Sean's toe.	_____ _____
4. Madeline said she would pinch Sean's pinky.	_____ _____
5. Madeline thought she found an earring.	_____ _____
6. _____ _____	Mrs. Gramme was startled.
7. _____ _____	Rosemary Ann Thyme's desk fell over.
8. _____ _____	The copy of *Hamlet* fell apart.

Extension: Write an ending for this story, answering such questions as: What does Madeline do? Where are the earrings?

Name _____

When East Met West

Miss Sabrina Sivix, a sixth grade social studies teacher, took her class to the computer lab a few days ago. She asked each student to prepare a report and time line on an important event in world history. Wes Kidd, whom some students tagged "Whiz Kidd," got to work immediately. He keyed-in a report on Marco Polo and Kublai Khan. Away he went! Here is Wes' report.

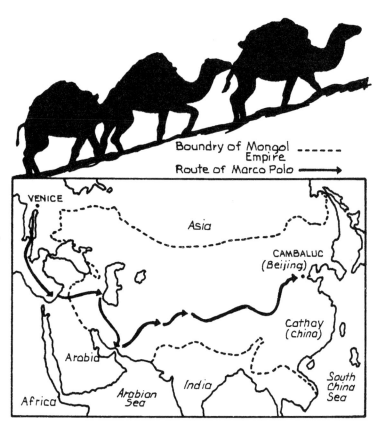

Boundry of Mongol Empire - - - - -
Route of Marco Polo ⟶

I have decided to report on two great people in world history: Kublai Khan, a Mongol ruler of China, and Marco Polo, a Venetian explorer and merchant. Their meeting in the 13th century is an early example of how East met West in world trade and government.

Kublai Khan became the Great-Khan of the Mongol empire in 1260. By 1266, he had gained control of the eastern Mongol territories. Kublai's brothers, the other descendants of the mighty Genghis Khan, did not respect Kublai's power and the Empire could not maintain its unity.

During this time, two Venetian merchant brothers, Nicolo and Maffeo Polo, traveled to China to trade goods from Europe and the Middle East. They were awed by the wealth of the khan and vastness of his land. They returned to Venice in 1269 with fascinating stories to share with their family. In 1271, they invited Nicolo's 17-year-old son Marco to join them on their second overland journey to the Far East. They arrived at Kublai Khan's summer palace in Shang-du in 1274.

For years, Marco Polo remained in China. Because Marco knew four languages, Kublai Khan entrusted him with many matters of state. Khan sent military expeditions to many parts of Southeast Asia. Twice he attempted to invade Japan, once in 1274 and again seven

years later, but these missions failed. In 1279 Khan completed his conquest of the southern Chinese Sung dynasty. Kublai improved cultural relations throughout the world.

Because the khan's rule was uncertain, the Polos thought it wise to return to Italy. They got their chance in 1292. When they arrived in Venice three years later, their city was at war with Genoa. Marco Polo was captured and jailed by the Genoese in 1296. While imprisoned, he dictated a book, called *Description of the World,* detailing his adventures in China.

Because the book described an amazing culture far distant from Europe, many critics considered it silly fantasy. As other merchant explorers returned with similar stories, Europeans slowly changed their thinking and accepted Marco Polo's tale.

Name _____

When East Met West

Help Wes complete this time line by writing in events to go with the dates shown below.

1260   _____

_____

1266   _____

_____

1269   _____

_____

1271   _____

_____

1274   _____

_____

1279   _____

_____

1292   _____

_____

1295   _____

_____

1296   _____

_____

Extension: Use reference materials to write a description of two other important events in the lives of Marco Polo or Kublai Khan.

Name _____

Odd One Out

Read each paragraph below. Then follow the directions on the next page.

1. Wes tried to comfort Sean about the class reaction. "They don't know anything! When Betsy spoke, she was just spinning wool about the jello. I know that you would never put orange jello on Mr. Tuit's chair. Anyway, you know Mr. Tuit, he has eyes in the back of his head. You'll see, the real criminal is going to get burned."

2. Bob shook his head sadly. "Your hand looks terrible. You should not let the poison ivy spread to either foot."

3. "Listen carefully for your positions, drama students. The queen must stand behind the parapet. No, no, a little further, Betsy. That's right. The count should come in from stage left. He sees the duchess weeping at the pool. Remember, Francesca, your dog is missing, so make those tears come! Now, the empress will come in from behind the audience. She should take everyone by surprise."

4. Here is Betsy Moss's poem:

    As sun arises in the east,
    I plod o'er streets and walks.
    While under earth a surly beast,
    Before its victim stalks.

5. During class detention, Francesca Fontaine thought about her crazy class-mates. She couldn't understand them. Why wouldn't all the students be quiet in class? And what is wrong with those three boys, Bob, Sean, and Wes? Don't they understand that they look silly when they wear their sunglasses upside down? Oh, well. Francesca shouldn't talk. Some-times she wears her retainer upside down.

6. "We saw a batch of ducklings hatch in the thatch without a scratch," explained Kyesha to Mrs. Wyze, the principal.

7. Henry Wadsworth Wordsmith stomped along disgustedly behind his classmates during the field trip to the farm. So what if Bob's aunt and uncle possessed horses. You couldn't practice your equestrian skills with them. And that cow was dis-gusting. It slobbered from its huge bovine mug while it chomped on its sickeningly pungent hay. No one, absolutely no one, could get Henry within 50 feet of that pig ever again, that muck-encrusted repulsive beast. Even the chickens with their red combs and proud demeanor couldn't alter Henry's adamant hatred for the "Bob Evansian Animal Kingdom."

Odd One Out

From page 20, read one paragraph at a time to complete the chart below. Find four examples of words that fit each category heading. Write those words in the "Examples" column. In the "Odd One Out" column, write the one word of the four you just listed that is somehow different from the other three. Explain how it is different in the "How Different" column. The seven odd words in the "Odd One Out" column can be arranged to form a familiar expression. Write the expression at the bottom of the page.

Category	Examples	Odd One Out	How Different?
1. personal pronouns			
2. four-letter words			
3. lordly folk			
4. prepositions			
5. contractions			
6. "atch" words			
7. farm animals			

Expression: _____

Games People Play

Betsy and her father squared off on either end of the kitchen table.

"Honey, I'm putting my foot down! You may not have a sleep-over," proclaimed Mr. Moss in his parental voice.

"But Dad, I only have kids over once in a blue moon. You won't have to go out of your way with a bunch of us girls here. You won't even hear us." Betsy forced six tears to roll down her cheeks and looked genuinely doleful.

At this, Anselm Moss perked up his ears. "Now don't try to pull my leg! How many kids would you invite? You know how I get cold feet at the mention of a sleep-over."

Betsy saw the crack in the door and reached to force it open. "Oh, Dad, I'd only have three or four friends over. We'll be as quiet as mice; you'll see. I see eye to eye with you about noise in the apartment. There won't be any loose cannon around here."

Papa looked at his offspring with trusting eyes. "Well, I'm glad to hear that. I hope this means I can wash my hands of any duties here. You'll take care of snacks and such, and see that the neighbors don't fuss?"

"Yup, I'll be on my toes. We'll foot the bill for it all. You'll see; I can stand on my own two feet. It'll be great!"

"Hon, you know you're the apple of my eye, but I can say no more parties 'til the cows come home. I just don't want a repeat performance of last year when your party got out of hand. We were only able to keep this apartment by the skin of our teeth."

"It's different now. I'm much more mature, you know. You'll see," assured Betsy with

her girl scout smile while Mr. Moss whistled to himself as he made his way to the den.

Betsy turned around. She was on cloud nine. She reached for the phone and dialed. "Hi, Francesca, the party's on for Friday night! Yeah, I know. He tried to be a wet blanket, but I stuck to my guns . . . I was skating on thin ice for a while, but everything's fine now. See ya!"

Name _____

Games People Play

The story on the previous page contains many idioms. Find 15 of them. Record them in the left column below and explain what each means in ordinary language on the right. You may find more than fifteen.

Idiom	In Ordinary Language

Name _____

Furry Things

Read these strange sentences and follow the directions on page 25.

1. At the two-family garage sale Tom bought a top, wheel, kite, hammer, and lamp stand.

2. "Bob was eating nuts for three days straight," complained Betsy.

3. Henry pulled the slot handle to one side as he reached for the grape gum ball.

4. In front of Betsy's mini cam, elephants wander about at the Toronto Zoo.

5. During the January blizzard, Sean howled, "Let's go attack the girls before they store any more snowball ammo."

6. "Yes, owing to my pained intestines I must leave school early," rationalized Henry mournfully.

7. "Watch my cousin Elmo leave his crib," snickered Francesca.

8. "Would you prefer pudding or jello?" inquired our super waiter.

9. "Use dry wood," chuckled Kyesha to Francesca as the girls prepared a camp-fire.

10. "Hey Dad, that pie sure would hit the spot terrifically for me," beamed Betsy.

11. "Mom, may we go to the Acadia Clam Bake?" questioned Shanda as they planned their Maine vacation.

12. A big horned beast stared out of the wildlife poster at Tom.

13. "That overgrown prickly hedge hogs the whole sidewalk," grumbled Henry.

14. "I dare ya to touch the hot pan. Dare, dare, double-dare," challenged Kyesha.

15. "Oww! A crab bit my toe!" howled Sean.

16. "A pear is the perfect fruit," purred Francesca to her pet kitten Sparkles.

17. "How did you do in geography, Ena?" asked Shanda.

18. "Never sob early in the morning, son!" warned Mrs. Evans.

19. "Oh, Momma, dat vas a bad germ," spouted Betsy in her short skit "The Guest."

20. "Are you a pole catcher?" Kyesha breathlessly asked a muscular sophomore pole-vaulter.

21. "Let's make Bob catcher for our team," suggested Sean.

22. "We'll name our chimp Alabama," decided Miss Sivix after much discussion.

23. "Leave the crib exactly where you found it," ordered Bob's mom as the two boys planned their fort design.

24. "Does this anchor seem heavy to you?" Wes asked Sean on their fishing trip.

25. "Please pardon key elements of my speech," Henry suggested.

26. "Let's put the toy box in that far attic corner," proposed Francesca.

27. Mr. Tuit stared at the Thanksgiving ham sternly. "Needs more time," he sighed.

28. "Is the sea like a big lake?" Bob's kid sister asked inquisitively.

Name _____

Furry Things

The sentences on the previous page have one thing in common; the name of a mammal is hidden within each sentence. For example, in the first sentence the words "wheel, kite" hide the word "elk" when we cross off the first and last letters (whe**el, k**ite). Write the name of each camouflaged critter.

1. _____

2. _____

3. _____

4. _____

5. _____

6. _____

7. _____

8. _____

9. _____

10. _____

11. _____

12. _____

13. _____

14. _____

15. _____

16. _____

17. _____

18. _____

19. _____

20. _____

21. _____

22. _____

23. _____

24. _____

25. _____

26. _____

27. _____

28. _____

Extension: Write your own sentences using these buggy words: gnat, butterfly, grasshopper, monarch, honeybee, wasp, damselfly, beetle, mantis, mayfly, ladybug, hornet, flea, swallowtail, ant, and bluebottle.

The Tree

Wesley Kidd walks home from school with his next door neighbor Annie. She is in the fifth grade and a bit of a tomboy. Both Annie and Wes like to play outdoors when the weather allows, and the tree behind their houses is the perfect place to play.

Wes, Annie, and the other neighbor kids love the tree. The overgrown monster of an apple tree stands alone in a field where an entire orchard once stood. The tree hadn't grown a decent apple for ages, but it was perfect for climbing. Three or four kids could scale its reaches and disappear from each other in its wondrous foliage. Some time back, Wes and Annie had tied a rope about eight feet up in one of its branches so they could hoist themselves up into the tree without climbing up the trunk.

"Nyaah, Wes! You can't get me!" called Annie from high in the tree. She stuck out her tongue teasingly.

"Why, you little shrimp," joked Wes. "I could catch you anytime, anywhere! You'd better climb higher than that 'cuz here I come."

Wes began pulling himself up the rope as he had done scores of times before. This time, though, his hands slipped from the rope, and down he fell.

As he tumbled to earth, Wes reached out to break his fall. His left arm slammed into an old wooden crate. Embarrassed by his fall, Wes sat up quickly and sheepishly glanced up toward Annie.

"Ah . . . Annie, you didn't . . . ah, see that, did you?"

"See that! Oh, man, you made firewood out of that crate. If you had chopped me like that, I'd be in a gazillion pieces." Annie seemed impressed.

Wes looked down. The crate was a mess. And his arm hurt a bit. Wes stood up and tried to climb the rope once more, but his arm hurt too much. He walked over to the trunk and began climbing the lower branches while favoring his arm.

"Ooh! He's alive, and he's dangerous. The ape man from Planet X is looking vicious," called Annie as she further ascended the airy arms of the tree. But as she glanced back at her friend, Wes wasn't moving from his perch in the lowest branches. His face told the story.

Annie knew he didn't want to cry in front of her. But he sure looked like he needed to.

"Hey, Dumbo," Annie teased to break the tension, "you better go home and have that arm checked out."

"Nah, it's all right," assured Wes. He knew she was right, but his tears were near the rim. "It's just a bruise."

"Wes," bossed Annie in the most serious voice she could produce, "now you get going. Tell your mom that your arm hurts. Tell her you think it's broken. She'll know what to do." Annie glared as only a bossy, caring friend could.

"Well, okay," sighed Wes.

He gingerly leapt from his low perch. Even this slight jolt pained his now throbbing arm. But no tears came. He won't allow them to come until he tells his mom, and maybe they wouldn't come then either. But it would be all right if he did cry; he was certain his arm was broken.

Name _____

The Tree

Sometimes we fear that others may think we are weak, or babies, or "sissies." Wes has some of these fears. Complete the columns by listing in what ways you think Wes appears weak, and in what ways he shows courage.

How Wes Appears Weak	How Wes Shows Courage

Conclusion: What do you conclude about Wesley? Is he a weak sissy, or is he strong? Explain.

_____

_____

_____

_____

_____

Extension: Hold a class discussion on how views of boys and girls have changed over time. What are some old taboos our society no longer holds for either males or females? Check with adults to get their ideas and impressions.

Name _____

Wet and Wild

Miss Sabrina Sivix, a 6th-grade social studies teacher, often encourages her students to work with partners as they research and prepare class presentations. Henry Wadsworth Wordsmith thought it would be convenient to work with Wes Kidd, the whiz kid, but Wes was already partnered with Sean. Henry decided to team up with Bob Evans.

Now Bob and Henry are as different as milk and orange juice. Henry's work is precise but dull, while Bob's work might be described as colorful and imaginative. Here is their report on the Nile River:

1   The Nile River of Africa is the longest river in the world. It stretches more than 4,100 miles and drains into the Mediterranean Sea.

2   Astronauts of Apollo 97, looking down from their spacecraft, could see the Nile from 100 million miles away. They said it looked like a blue earthworm. Commander Burt Runbolt said, "Yup, it's shore purty. And it slithers from side to side like a wiggly worm too!"

3   Tributaries of the Nile River include the Atbara, the Blue Nile, and the White Nile. The White Nile obtains much of its water from Lake Albert and Lake Victoria, the latter of which is the largest lake in Africa. The While Nile and the Blue Nile combine around Khartoum, Sudan, and proceed northward to Lake Nasser in southern Egypt.

4   Many wonderful creatures live in and near the Nile River. Crocodiles, snakes, and frogs are plentiful. The Nile region also includes numerous sheep led by peculiar rams. Some books spell these animal's names incorrectly. They call them Ramses instead of rams. A couple of these large and powerful males were such great leaders that they could convince whole armies of Egyptians to fight for them. They must have been able to communicate with humans. Can you believe it? Another creature of the Nile is the hippopotamus. Sometimes whole herds of them would flop into the river and flood vast plains further downstream, killing people and livestock.

5   People living along the Nile River have many different jobs. Some people fish, others are cultivators of the soil, while still others raise cattle and camels.

6   An amazing engineering project in modern history is the Aswan High Dam, completed in 1970. This mammoth structure, filled with rocks, is 17 times the volume of the Great Pyramid at Giza. The dam provides hydroelectric power to much of Egypt. It also allows for agricultural expansion for the country.

7   That's about all we have to say about the Nile. We'd like to add that America's ties to Egypt are very close today. Two large American companies, the Cairo Syrup Foundation and Delta Airlines, were started by Egyptian business people. Their names were Ms. Anne Warsadat and Mr. Moe Barek.

Name _____

Wet and Wild

Henry writes only facts while Bob loves to
fantasize. List the paragraphs that would
most likely be written by each boy?

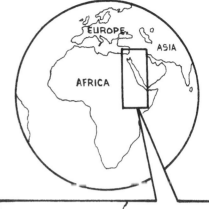

Henry _____

Bob _____

List five factual details from the boys' report.

_____

_____

_____

_____

_____

List five fictitious details from the same report.

_____

_____

_____

_____

_____

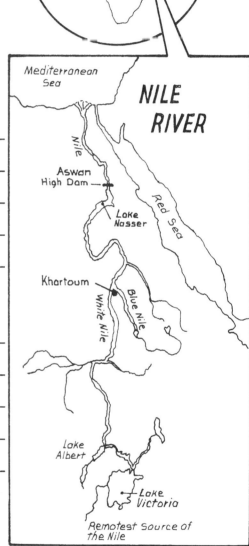

Extension: Write a paragraph that includes two truths and one zany lie about one of the following topics: ancient Athens, ancient China, the Vikings, the Congo, or the Incas.

Memories

"Tommy? Is that you, child?" It was Grandma's voice. Grandma had moved back to the farmhouse, her homestead, when Grandpa died last year. She often sat in her rocker in the sunroom. Sometimes she worked with her stitchery there, although she often complained that her eyes were going bad.

"Yeah, Grandma. It's me." Tom walked into the sunroom. Grandma was rocking. Her hands were on her lap. She was staring out the window. No one farmed here any more. There wasn't enough money in farming these days. Tom's dad worked for a trucking service, and his mom was an accountant in town. But the family still owned the farmland and all the buildings. Now Grandma was gazing in the direction of the paint-flecked barn.

"I remember milking the cows, Tommy. I remember we'd start afternoon chores about now. There'd be four of us milking, because we had to do it by hand."

Tom sat down at his grandmother's feet. He didn't remember the farm animals; they, with all the farm equipment, had been sold off long before he had been born. "Didn't you ever own a milking machine, Grandma?"

"No." Grandma smiled, and her eyes turned misty. "No, our hands were our machines. Grandpa and I figured it was a waste of fool money to buy such an extravagance."

She patted Tom on the head. There was a pause as Grandma set her hands back in her lap. "We pretty well knew your mom wasn't going to take over the business and your pa was no farmer, though he's a good lad. And when Hank died, well, a bit of all of us died too."

Tom had heard of Uncle Hank, Mom's younger brother. He had joined the Marines, but never returned home. One day the government sent two military personnel out to the farm—about the time Tommy was a toddler—and an officer told the family that Uncle Hank had died in a freak accident.

"Grandma, would you like to see the farm again?"

"Tommy, I do see the farm, every day."

"I know, but would you like to see cows and chickens and pigs again?"

During the pause which followed, Tom heard a mourning dove coo its sad song. "Yes boy, I would. I miss the sounds and smells of a busy farm."

Tom silently left the room, leaving his grandmother alone with her memories. The rocker creaked on the oval, rag rug. In a few minutes, Tom was back. "Grandma, where's your blue sweater? Mom's coming home early so we can take you to the Eerdman's farm. They just started milking."

Skill: Vocabulary

Name _____

Memories

Find words in the story that match the words or phrases below. When you finish, the letters in the boxes will spell out a phrase.

1. grieving   __ __ __ ☐ __ __ __ __

2. recall   __ __ __ ☐ __ __

3. materials, machinery   __ __ __ __ ☐ __ __ __ __

4. stroked   __ __ __ ☐ __ __

5. one who works the land   __ __ __ ☐ __ __

6. answers "why?"   ☐ __ __ __ __ __ __

7. farmhouse   __ __ ☐ __ __ __ __ __

8. needlework   __ __ __ __ __ __ ☐ __

9. finance record-keeper   __ __ __ __ __ ☐ __ __

10. child learning to walk   __ __ __ __ ☐ __ __

11. quietly   __ __ ☐ __ __ __ __

12. fragile   ☐ __ __ __ __

13. bird call   __ ☐ __

14. boy   ☐ __ __

15. unusual   __ __ __ ☐ __

16. gazing   ☐ __ __ __ __ __ __

Extension: Write to or talk with your grandparents about their lives. Write down some of their stories. Visit homes of elderly people you know.

Name _____

A Long Way Off

Mr. Ron Tuit, a sixth grade science teacher, zealously introduced astronomical distance to his students. Then he sent them to the media center. Their job: Discover how far certain stars are from Earth. Kyesha reminded the class that a light year is the distance light travels in one year, about 6 trillion miles.

Francesca learned that the star Lalande 21185 was about 8.1 light years away. The learner leapt lightly while loving the limelight as she alerted all lads and lasses to the fact.

Sean surveyed Sirius A and saw that its distance was 8.6 light years from this soil. Solemnly he said he was impressed by this discovery.

Betsy browsed boldly through the B books. She bubbled with bravado and broadcast that Barnard's Star blinked about 5.9 light years away.

Kyesha scoured science books to see that three stars, Alpha Centauri A, B, and C, were similar. They stood 4.3 light years from our significant solar system.

Henry hovered over the heading "Ross 248." This heavenly mass hung out at 10.5 light years. Henry howled haughty hurrahs.

Shanda shook her shaggy, shampoo-shimmering head of hair as she showed her sharp stats. "Luyten 726-8A is 8.9 light years off . . . Oh, and Luyten 726-8B is as well," she shared in shock.

Wes whistled as he worked wisely on Wolf 359. "Yes," he whispered. It was well away at 7.6 light years.

Saul tenaciously attacked his task to testify that light from Sirius B and Sirius A, took the same time — 8.6 light years — to travel to Earth.

Bob bungled badly until he briefed the class about Ross 154. What a bargain! "It blazes about 9.4 light years off!" he bellowed boisterously.

A Long Way Off

Using data collected from the class, complete the graph below. You will need to write in the name of each star and graph its distance from our solar system.

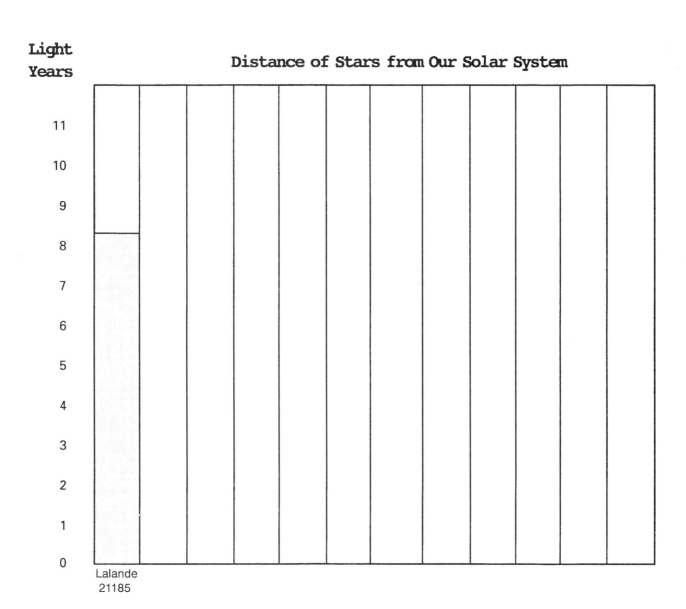

Light Years

Distance of Stars from Our Solar System

11
10
9
8
7
6
5
4
3
2
1
0

Lalande 21185

Extension: Write an explanation of the chart data using comparative language.

Muddy-Muck-Muck

"Hey, what's the matter with you? Why'd ya push me into the swamp?" Bob sputtered at Tom as he raised a muddied fist in the air.

"I . . . I . . . I th . . . thought you were playing the game with the rest of us," stammered Tom.

"Game? Yeah, right. Like this is part of our game!" Bob turned to his friend. "Hey, Henry, see what Tom did to me? He pushed me into the swamp! Probably ruined my brand new pumps."

"Why'd you push him in? You some kind of bully, Tom? I'm telling Mrs. Gramme what you did. Ooh, boy, wait 'til you get a load of the punishment she'll give you!" Henry pulled Bob from the muck and together they stomped off along the boardwalk. Henry turned to glare at Tom, but Tom wasn't looking.

The boys were at a fall weekend camp in a state forest reserve. Mrs. Gramme and her husband periodicallly ran weekend camps for kids from the school district. They liked to see students interact with each other as they experienced nature.

Tom stood still. Though his face was expressionless, Tom's mind was spinning. He stared out over the cattails to the smooth pond where a duck and her babies paddled.

"Hey, what's up, Tom? Aren't you playing anymore?" Sean dashed down the boardwalk to Tom. Wes came galloping behind him.

"I . . . I g-g got into trouble, Sean. I p-pushed Bob into the swamp."

"Of course you did, Tom. That's why we call this game muddy-muck-muck. Bob knows that. Good grief! He knocked Wes in just a few minutes ago."

"He did?"

"Yeah," Wes grinned. "I was in muck all the way up to my waist. See? I bet I got a quart of it in my shoes. Good thing I have clean clothes in the cabin."

Tom studied Wes' clothes. It was true enough. "Then why was Bob angry with me? He and Henry were both yelling something fierce."

"Forget about it," soothed Sean. "Bob just went off the deep end, and Henry followed him there."

"But they said they were going to tell Mrs. Gramme and that I'd be in big trouble." Sean and Wes roared at Tom's words. Wes put his arm on Tom's shoulder as Sean explained.

"Ah . . . Tom, guess who named the game muddy-muck-muck—Mrs. Gramme! She got tired of kids who'd come out here and lock themselves up in their cabins when they could be enjoying nature. She said a little mud never hurt anyone. You're not in trouble with Mrs. Gramme."

"That's right," said Wes. "If anyone's in trouble, it's Bob for alarming you. Hey, look! Is that a mother duck with her ducklings?"

"Yeah," said Tom. "She's teaching them how to swim and dive. See? She really takes good care of them."

"And we try to take care of each other," said Sean. "Okay?"

Muddy–Muck–Muck

Match the adjectives below to the boy(s) you think they best describe. Write each word in the appropriate circle. Be ready to defend your decision.

Word Bank				
friendly	compassionate	angry	puzzled	bullish
fearful	understanding	defensive	cowardly	horrified
kind	thoughtful	happy	wise	obstinate
offensive	selfish	helpful	rude	threatening

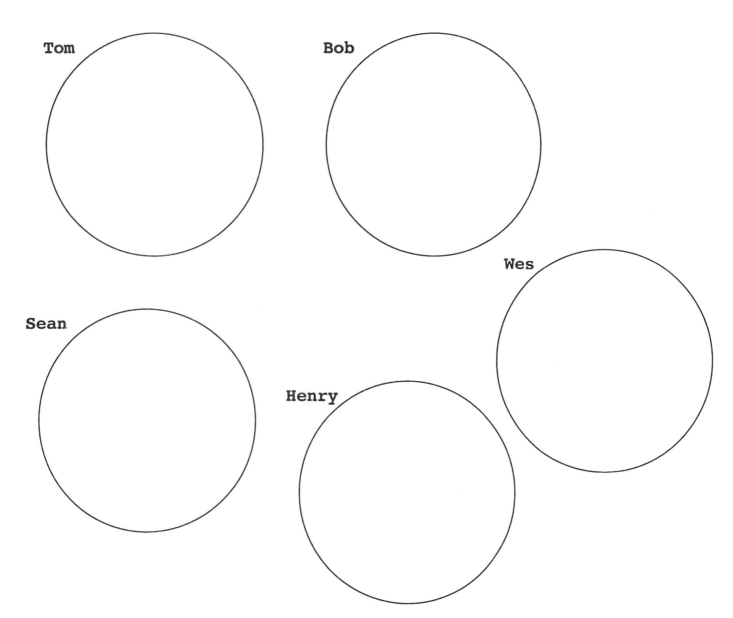

Extension: Act out one of these adjectives and have your classmates guess which one you have in mind.

Name _____

Scavenger Hunt

Shanda and Bob went on a bike ride one Saturday afternoon. They read all these different signs, posters, bumper stickers, and advertisements along the way.

HONK if you love Elvis!

Terrace Boulevard

COME SEE ♪ The ♪ Music ♪ Man
August 11-15

STU'S SHOES
Our penny loafers ain't cheap

TRY OUR MOUTH-WATERING
AVOCADO MAYONNAISE

Dr. Nipsy
Tastes smooth, less filling...
ONLY 5 CALORIES PER BOTTLE

YIELD RIGHT OF WAY

Mary Tsoski for School Board

SHOW PRIDE ☆☆☆☆☆☆☆ BUY AMERICAN

SPEED 30 M.P.H. LIMIT

5TH FEDERAL BANK YES, WE CARE

◁ Kaline Ball Park 2 blocks

IGLOO SCHOOL DISTRICT BUS #14

CITY OF **ENGLEWOOD**
SWEAT SOCK CAPITAL OF THE WORLD

COME TO **PAUL BUNYAN DAYS!**
CHOP TILL YOU DROP

TANTE'S STRUDELHAUS
Sehr gut!

WZZZ- THE STATION THAT PUTS YOU TO SLEEP

HEIMLICH MEDICAL CENTER
▪▬ 3 BLOCKS AFTER LIGHT ➡

PARK CLOSES AT DUSK

I ♡ TURTLES

Name _____

Scavenger Hunt

Use the signs on the previous page to answer the following questions.

1. What was the speed limit? _____

2. What was the name of the ball park? _____

3. What is "less filling?" _____

4. What street did they find? _____

5. What flavor of mayonnaise was advertised? _____

6. When was *The Music Man* showing? _____

7. What was the radio station's slogan? _____

8. What is "sehr gut?" _____

9. What is Number 14? _____

10. Who is Mary Tsoski? _____

11. What is the name of the Med Center? _____

12. What is Englewood's proud title? _____

13. What "ain't cheap?" _____

14. When should you honk? _____

15. What is the fifth? _____

16. What is the last word on the Bunyan sign? _____

17. How many signs are listed? _____

18. How many signs have only four words? _____

Extension: In your town, try to find the following signs and give their locations: a sign that has a number between 10 and 100, one which names an animal, one which names a person, and one bumper sticker.

Name _____

Snowball

When Henry Wadsworth Wordsmith was small, his mother allowed him to buy a cat. He wanted a dog; a boxer named Rusty, to be specific. Instead he got a cat. Henry turned six on the day the cat arrived. His mother insisted Henry wear a white shirt and tie and blue shorts with suspenders. Henry felt foolish, but he obeyed his mother. As soon as Mrs. Wordsmith placed the feline in Henry's lap, he marveled at this gift. It didn't matter that the cat's claws scratched his knees or that the poor beast clung to his neck when the neighbors' dog barked its welcome at the front door; she belonged to him. "I love you," Henry whispered.

Henry named his cat Snowball. She had gray eyes and pure white fur which fluffed out like a cat from a van Gogh painting. Her paws were so soft and tender, and she purred when Henry stroked her. She was quite large, almost too heavy for Henry to hold, but not quite. Murmuring into her fur, Henry would say, "Snowball, I really love you."

Snowball and Henry liked to play a game. Henry would open all the drawers in his dresser. He would then hide Snowball in one of the drawers. Snowball would scoot immediately into Henry's sock drawer. That was her home base. It didn't matter which of the six drawers Henry put her in, she would find her way to the socks. "She's so-oo smart," Henry bragged.

He fed her well. Mrs. Wordsmith bought powdered milk, and Henry mixed a fresh batch twice a day. Sometimes his mother allowed him to feed her tuna. But Snowball wasn't fussy; she would eat vegetables and fruit from Henry's hand as readily as fish. Mrs. Wordsmith called her "a maligned misfit of mediocre intelligence." Henry could tell that his mom was impressed.

Snowball knew when school was out. She'd always wait in the maple tree outside Henry's front door. As he'd turn up the front walk, she'd meow, scamper down the tree trunk, and throw herself into his stomach. Henry always caught her. "I love you like crazy," he'd say.

Mrs. Wordsmith said that Snowball was a thermo-crazy feline. She would sit in front of the clothes drier vent, in the sun on simmering, hot days, or near the oven when bread was baking. Snowball discovered that recently driven cars gave heat as well. She rested in wheel wells to soak in the radiating heat from a car engine. "What a nut," beamed Henry. "I love you, Snowball!"

One day Snowball didn't jump down from her perch in the tree to greet Henry on his arrival home. She slid from behind a bush. She didn't walk straight either, but stepped sideways toward Henry so he could see only her left side. When she meowed, her mouth moved funny.

Henry got down on his haunches. "Hey, Snowball, you got a new trick, girl?" But she didn't. The right side of her body was damaged.

Henry's mother had to put her to sleep that night. "Too much pain," she said.

"Too much pain!" cried Henry. He promised he would never love anything again.

Name _____

Snowball

Answer these questions.

1. What kind of parent do you imagine Mrs. Wordsmith is? List three clues.

   _____

   _____

   _____

2. *Snowball* is a simple name. What might be a more humorous name? . . .a more regal name? . . .a more prophetic name?

   _____

   _____

3. What other games might a six-year-old boy play with his cat?

   _____

   _____

4. How do you imagine the cat was injured? Explain.

   _____

   _____

5. Other than a pet's death, what events might cause a child to feel like Henry did at the end of *Snowball.*

   _____

   _____

6. How might Mrs. Wordsmith best help her son following the cat's death? Explain.

   _____

   _____

   _____

Extension: In one or two paragraphs describe either 1) a painful experience you had or 2) a painful experience you could have had.

FOLKLORE NEWSPAPER

VOL IV   1996

As you read each news article, think about the main idea.

1. It was a great shock to me. You know, the story of Rapunzel who was nabbed by an evil witch. Do you remember her long hair? Well, hold your britches. The scoop is that it really wasn't her own hair. No siree! It seems she and the witchy-poo had a wig business going for nigh unto five years. I always wondered how anyone could grow hair as long as that.

2. Don't tell me you believed that story about the wicked wolf blowing down the houses of two of the three little pigs? That's hogwash. I mean, have you ever tried blowing down even a one-foot pile of sticks? Hard to imagine. Now *Folklore Newspaper* has heard from reliable, but anonymous sources, that the wolf purchased seven powerful electric fans. That is the only reasonable solution short of a tornado. Seriously.

3. Ever hear of Mattie Habler? Probably not. Over time, people have given her the handle Mother Hubbard. Why? Well, we don't know. We can only imagine it's because Hubbard rhymes with cupboard. After all, Mattie was no one's mother. Shoot! She was a mean-spirited, hateful hag, and she was finally kicked out of Gooseberg when she starved that poor dog. No one has heard from her since. And there's no truth to her lookin' in her cupboard for dog biscuits or puppy food with the poor pooch pawing at her feet. The dog, a long, thin St. Bernard, was kept chained in a minuscule pen in her backyard. No love lost between those two, let me tell ya.

4. Bob Horner's kid, Jack, was one mischievous little rascal. Ol' Bob never knew quite what to do with that boy. Seems whenever I'd go over for a game of checkers, the boy would either be confined in his room for some transgression, or he'd be sittin' in the kitchen corner. That Jack! He had this wonderful grin and the prettiest twinkle in his eyes. Bob could never stay angry with him for long. One time the nervy kid dipped his thumb into a freshly baked cherry pie (no plums at Christmas for him) right in front of his pa. Then he smiled and said, "I'm a good boy, I am, huh, da?" Old Bob just rolled his eyes and shook his head.

5. The poor troll in the Norse tale of the billy goats really gets rippped off. Here he is taking a swim in the river and just as he's pulling himself onto the bridge to dry, that pesky little goat comes prancing over. The troll is so surprised that he falls back in, losing his brand-new flippers. Then just as he's pulling himself up the second time, the medium-sized goat steps on this hands and back into the river he goes! As you can imagine, the sight of the third goat scared the short, bearded fellow so much he just plain gave up. He dove into the water and swam away downstream. I still have the shoes he left on the bridge. And that's the truth.

Name _____

Folklore Newspaper

Write an appropriate headline for each story from the *Folklore Newspaper.* The attention-grabbing headline should fit the tone and main idea of the story.

1. _____

   _____

2. _____

   _____

3. _____

   _____

4. _____

   _____

5. _____

   _____

Choose one of the following headlines and write a news story expressing your interpretation of the fairy tale.

   ·Woodcutter and Hermit Grandmother Charged with Animal Cruelty
   ·Giant's Home Burglarized by Unruly Teen

_____

_____

_____

_____

_____

_____

_____

Name _____

Roughing It?

When the four girls decided to take a short camping trip, Kyesha, with a twinkle in her eye, gave a daring suggestion. Why not have a NO-PLAN campout? Each girl grabs whatever she thinks the group needs. If the group runs short of something, no problem. It's just a one-nighter anyway.

At noon the following day, Mr. Moss dropped the girls off at rustic Bowman's Lake. The girls hiked down the trail to the clearing where Betsy's family had camped before. Each girl took two trips to bring the supplies to their site. As they un-loaded, the girls discovered they had more than enough of many things. Shanda and Francesca both brought potato chips; Francesca and Kyesha had each hauled a small propane camp stove. The other girls laughed when Betsy held up three rolls of toilet paper. "Well, I have to blow my nose a lot when I camp," she said indignantly. But she smiled too.

Francesca brought her family's six-person tent. When the girls set it up, they discovered that the stakes were missing. "Oh, my dumb brother probably borrowed it for one of his inventions," Francesca moaned.

"No problem," comforted Shanda. She and Betsy had each brought a Swiss army knife, and in a short time the two had whittled enough stakes for the tent.

Each girl had brought her own sleeping bag and air mattress. Since no one remembered an air pump, the girls inflated the mattresses the old-fashioned way. "Whew! This is tiring me out," moaned Shanda after ten minutes.

Kyesha glanced over at Shanda's handiwork. "Shanda, you've got problems, girl. There's a big hole in your air mattress."

"Did anyone bring patches?" asked Shanda hopefully. The girls slowly shook their heads.

"Well, what's for supper then?" cried Shanda. "Let's feast my blues away."

Betsy smiled, "We've got 20 hot dogs, 16 buns, two jars of ketchup, a can of peas. . ."

"Skip the peas," laughed Francesca. "I don't want any; not when I've brought dessert." She reached into a box she had painstakingly carried from town. In it was a pan of fudge, a blueberry pie, and a large bag of trail mix.

So, ignoring all other foods, the girls sat around eating Francesca's fortifying feast. They washed it all down with two large bottles of cola. Eventually they tired of eating and decided to play cards and Clue.

Toward evening, Shanda jumped up from the ground. "All right, everyone. It's time for Camp Croquet." She pulled out 4 croquet balls and 10 wickets.

"Where are the mallets?" asked Betsy.

"Who needs mallets? We'll improvise!" shouted Shanda. She grabbed a branch off the forest floor. Betsy did likewise. Francesca shrugged and grabbed the camp shovel. Kyesha finally settled for her pillow.

"It's hard enough anyway," she remarked positively.

The girls played until dark. Then they hiked off into the woods carrying their hot dogs, chips, and pop. Since no one had a flashlight, they stumbled a lot. They joked when they learned that each of them had remembered two books of matches.

Gathering around a small fire, the girls roasted hot dogs and marshmallows. When an owl hooted nearby, Betsy whispered, "Not bad, not bad at all."

Name _____

Roughing It?

List the items the girls brought (or forgot to bring) on the campout under the appropriate category heading.

Food

_____
_____
_____
_____
_____
_____
_____

Camp Supplies

_____
_____
_____
_____
_____
_____
_____

Games

_____
_____
_____
_____
_____
_____
_____

Forgot to Bring

_____
_____
_____
_____
_____
_____
_____

Extension: Write a camp-out story where one of the following happens: 1) someone becomes lost in the woods, 2) a bug crawls into someone's ear, 3) a camper walks in his sleep, or 4) raccoons steal the food.

Answer Key
Reading Comprehension
Grade 6

Skill: Story Mapping

Name _____

Accidents Do Happen

Main Character: Sean D. Keene

Setting: school, then home

Problem: An accident-prone Sean must complete a school assignment and many tasks at home.

Key Events:
1. Sean finds out that he is unprepared for the homework assignment due tomorrow.
2. Sean pinched his finger in the nutcracker.
3. He tears out his old tree fort and hurts himself with a crowbar.
4. He uses a broom to clean up the debris on the driveway and breaks his arm.
5. Sean shared the details of his day in class, but is praised for completing his school work.

Solution to problem: Sean's real-life experiences with tools fit the classroom assignment.

Evaluation: Sean didn't really complete his assignment— he was lucky.   Answers will vary.

Extension: Draw pictures to illustrate the 3 lever types. Use words such as fulcrum, force, and load. List examples of each from the story.

Skill: Reading for Details

Name _____

Mow-'Em-Down

Mrs. Gramme was so pleased with Francesca's report that she made copies of the report along with a list of questions to be answered by the entire class. See if you can answer these questions too.

1. How do we know from this biography that Matt Mulroney is a strong man? (3 ways)

    He held the get-away vehicle after a robbery. His muscles are evident because his nickname is "the Ripple." He plowed through five opponents.

2. List three phrases that describe Mr. Mulroney's visual appearance. Answers may vary.

    chipped tooth, smokey-brown eyes, 6'4" 297 lbs, muscular, long, black hair, large feet

3. In what way has Mow-'Em-Down been lucky?
    The get-away truck could not shift into reverse.

4. Tell what position Matt played on the team.
    defensive lineman

5. Underline the adjectives that best describe Matt Mulroney.

brave	<u>popular</u>	fearful
vicious	<u>handsome</u>	hard-working
short	blond	<u>muscular</u>
intelligent	sickly	<u>fortunate</u>

Skill: Central and Supporting Statements

Name _____

A Royal Pain

Write the central statement of the report in the center of the web. Then list four supporting statements. Finally, give the details that clarify each supporting statement.

Supporting Statement: He never really grew up.

Details: He fought with his family. He couldn't sit still. -selfish

Supporting Statement: He ruled poorly.

Details: He spent only 6 months in England. He left the care of England to others.

Central Statement: King Richard I was not a great ruler.

Supporting Statement: He cost England a fortune.

Details: Wars cost a fortune. The Romans demanded a huge ransom for Richard.

Supporting Statement: He lost English-held land to France.

Details: During his imprisonment France seized English land.

Extension: Research the Crusades. Find out why they were fought; who fought them; and what the results were.

Metropolis

Name _____

Betsy made less of a muddle with her notes when she completed the following chart. Use the clues from page 8 to organize the city information according to size.

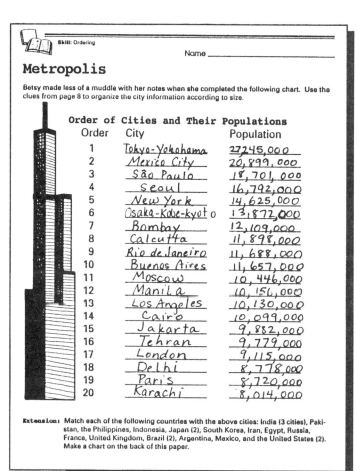

Order of Cities and Their Populations

Order	City	Population
1	Tokyo-Yokohama	27,245,000
2	Mexico City	20,899,000
3	São Paulo	18,701,000
4	Seoul	16,792,000
5	New York	14,625,000
6	Osaka-Kobe-kyoto	13,872,000
7	Bombay	12,109,000
8	Calcutta	11,898,000
9	Rio de Janeiro	11,688,000
10	Buenos Aires	11,657,000
11	Moscow	10,446,000
12	Manila	10,156,000
13	Los Angeles	10,130,000
14	Cairo	10,099,000
15	Jakarta	9,882,000
16	Tehran	9,779,000
17	London	9,115,000
18	Delhi	8,778,000
19	Paris	8,720,000
20	Karachi	8,014,000

Extension: Match each of the following countries with the above cities: India (3 cities), Pakistan, the Philippines, Indonesia, Japan (2), South Korea, Iran, Egypt, Russia, France, United Kingdom, Brazil (2), Argentina, Mexico, and the United States (2). Make a chart on the back of this paper.

A Special Attraction

Name _____

Answer these questions.

1. Why might Tom be attracted to Shanda? Give two plausible explanations.

   Answers will vary.

2. What might cause Tom to be shy or withdrawn? Give three plausible explanations.

   Answers will vary.

3. How does Shanda show a caring nature?

   She tried to start a conversation with Tom. She was respectful toward Tom even when he was shy and nervous.

4. Imagine that the conversation at the end of the story continues. How might you complete it?

   Accept reasonable responses.

Extension: Why do you think some people are more affectionate toward animals than others?

They're All As

Name _____

Write the letter of the correct meaning on the line to match each of the words from the story.

C agouti — a. disgusting
a abhorrent — b. without purpose
e amicable — c. rodent
f anguish — d. clay
h adjourned — e. friendly
g acerbic — f. distress
b aimless — g. harsh
d adobe — h. dismissed

g arbor — a. like an uncle
a avuncular — b. similar
f adulation — c. frightened
c alarmed — d. isolation
h assist — e. changed
d alienation — f. praise
b akin — g. shady place
e altered — h. help

g abruptly — a. compressed
e alluded — b. insult
a abridged — c. lofty
b affront — d. undertaking
h agenda — e. hinted
d adventure — f. unite
f affiliate — g. without warning
c aerial — h. plan

c apt — a. bordered
a abutted — b. sore
d adage — c. likely
e archaic — d. saying
f aggregate — e. old
g abode — f. total
b abscess — g. dwelling

Kids Say the Darndest Things

Name _____

Match quotes from the previous page with the emotions they project. Use each quote only once.

On receiving homework...
worried A4   disgusted A3
hopeful A1   bewildered A2

On dissecting earthworms...
enthusiastic B3   adamant B1
sympathetic B2   generous B4

On losing a ball game...
embarrassed C1   angry C4
fearful C2   tired C3

On having a special assembly...
joking D1   excited D4
awed D3   bored D2

On opening one's lunch...
surprised E2   satisfied E3
disappointed E4   doubtful E1

Extension: Choose one of the themes from the reading selection. Decide the emotions you would like to project. Write a dialogue to convey those feelings. You may use part of the quotes shown, but you must expand to create a full converstion.

Wherefore Art Thou?

Skill: Cause and Effect

Name _____

Madeline caused a chain reaction of unfortunate events. Complete the cause and the effect statement pairs below.

Cause	Effect
1. Mrs. Gramme wanted to demonstrate medieval head gear.	Mrs. Gramme removed her earrings.
2. Mrs. Gramme wanted to search for her earrings.	Mrs. Gramme asked the class to read quietly.
3. Madeline stepped on Sean's toe.	Sean squelched a scream and said, "What are you doing?"
4. Madeline said she would pinch Sean's pinky.	Sean stilled immediately.
5. Madeline thought she found an earring.	She shouted and pointed under the desk.
6. Madeline shouted, "There it is!"	Mrs. Gramme was startled.
7. Mrs. Gramme jumped and fell into Rosemary's desk.	Rosemary Ann Thyme's desk fell over.
8. Rosemary's book sailed to the floor.	The copy of *Hamlet* fell apart.

Extension: Write an ending for this story, answering such questions as: What does Madeline do? Where are the earrings?

Page 17

When East Met West

Skill: Sequence/Time Line

Name _____

Help Wes complete this time line by writing in events to go with the dates shown below.

1260 — Kublai Khan became the Great Khan of the Mongol empire.

1266 — He had gained control of the eastern Mongol territories.

1269 — Two merchants, Nicolo and Maffeo Polo, returned to Venice with exciting stories of the East.

1271 — The merchants returned to the Far East with Marco Polo.

1274 — The travelers arrived at Kublai Khan's summer palace in Shang-du.

1279 — Khan completed his conquest of the southern Chinese Sung dynasty.

1292 — The Polos left because Khan's rule seemed uncertain.

1295 — They arrived in Venice after a 3-year journey to find their city at war.

1296 — Marco Polo was captured and jailed by the Genoese. He starts writing.

Extension: Use reference materials to write a description of two other important events in the lives of Marco Polo or Kublai Khan.

Page 19

Odd One Out

Skill: Classifying

Name _____

From page 20, read one paragraph at a time to complete the chart below. Find four examples of words that fit each category heading. Write those words in the "Examples" column. In the "Odd One Out" column, write the one word of the four you just listed that is somehow different from the other three. Explain how it is different in the "How Different" column. The seven odd words in the "Odd One Out" column can be arranged to form a familiar expression. Write the expression at the bottom of the page.

Category	Examples	Odd One Out	How Different?
1 personal pronouns	they, she, you, he	they	plural pronoun
2 four-letter words	head, hand, your, foot	your	not part of the body
3 lordly folk	queen, count, duchess, empress	count	male term
4 prepositions	in, o'er, under, before	before	begins with a consonant
5 contractions	couldn't wouldn't shouldn't don't	don't	doesn't rhyme
6 "atch" words	batch, hatch, thatch, scratch	hatch	only verb
7 farm animals	horses, cow, pig, chickens	chickens	bird or 2-legged

Expression: Don't count your chickens before they hatch.

Page 21

Games People Play

Skill: Figurative Language

Name _____

The story on the previous page contains many idioms. Find 15 of them. Record them in the left column below and explain what each means in ordinary language on the right. You may find more than fifteen.

Idiom	In Ordinary Language
putting my foot down	being firm
once in a blue moon	very rarely
go out of your way	take special trouble
perked up his ears	His attention was roused.
pull my leg	fool me
cold feet	become nervous
crack in the door	opportunity
quiet as mice	quiet
see eye to eye	agree
loose cannon	wild behavior
wash my hands	take no responsibility
on my toes	alert
foot the bill	pay for it (responsible)
stand on my own two feet	be independent
apple of my eye	very precious
'til the cows come home	never
skin of our teeth	barely
cloud nine	pure bliss
wet blanket	discouraging person
stuck to my guns	firm in plans
skating on thin ice	close to failure

Page 23

Furry Things

Name _____

The sentences on the previous page have one thing in common; the name of a mammal is hidden within each sentence. For example, in the first sentence the words "wheel, kite" hide the word "elk" when we cross off the first and last letters (wh**el**, **k**ite). Write the name of each camouflaged critter.

1. elk
2. gnu
3. sloth
4. camel
5. goat
6. sow
7. mole
8. dingo
9. woodchuck
10. otter
11. lamb
12. bighorn
13. hedgehog
14. panda

15. rabbit
16. ape
17. hyena
18. bear
19. badger
20. polecat
21. bobcat
22. impala
23. ibex
24. horse
25. donkey
26. rat
27. hamster
28. seal

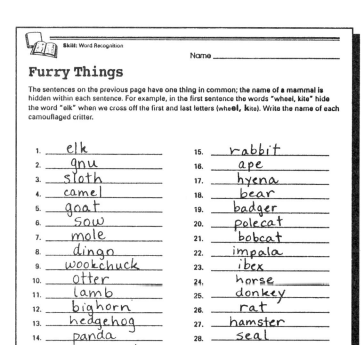

Extension: Write your own sentences using these buggy words: gnat, butterfly, grasshopper, monarch, honeybee, wasp, damselfly, beetle, mantis, mayfly, ladybug, hornet, flea, swallowtail, ant, and bluebottle.

Page 25

The Tree

Name _____

Sometimes we fear that others may think we are weak, or babies, or "sissies." Wes has some of these fears. Complete the columns by listing in what ways you think Wes appears weak, and in what ways he shows courage.

How Wes Appears Weak	How Wes Shows Courage
He walks home from school and plays with a girl.	He doesn't complain about walking with a younger girl.
Annie teases him.	He likes to play outside.
He is embarrassed by his fall.	He challenges Annie.
His face shows his pain.	He breaks a crate.
He nearly cries in public.	He climbs into the tree even with a hurt arm.
	He doesn't cry.

Conclusion: What do you conclude about Wesley? Is he a weak sissy, or is he strong? Explain.

Accept reasonable answers.

Extension: Hold a class discussion on how views of boys and girls have changed over time. What are some old taboos our society no longer holds for either males or females? Check with adults to get their ideas and impressions.

Page 27

Wet and Wild

Name _____

Henry writes only facts while Bob loves to fantasize. List the paragraphs that would most likely be written by each boy?

Henry   1, 3, 5, 6

Bob   2, 4, 7

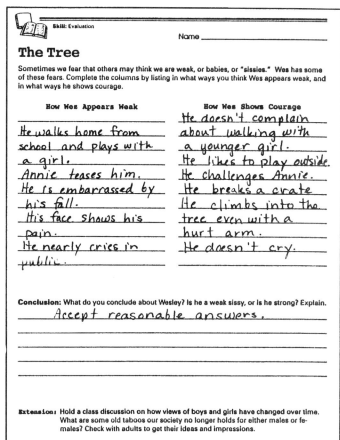

NILE RIVER

List five factual details from the boys' report.

The Nile River is 4,100 miles long. It drains into the Mediterranean. Tributaries include Atbara, Blue Nile, and White Nile. Lake Victoria is the largest lake in Africa. Jobs include farmers and fishermen. Aswan High Dam facts

List five fictitious details from the same report.

Apollo 97, 100 million miles, Burt Runbolt, Ramses is a misspelling of rams. Hippopotami flood the plains. Cairo Syrup and Delta Airlines are Egyptian. Its leaders are Ms. Anne Warsadat and Mr. Moe Barek.

Extension: Write a paragraph that includes two truths and one zany lie about one of the following topics: ancient Athens, ancient China, the Vikings, the Congo, or the Incas.

Page 29

Memories

Name _____

Find words in the story that match the words or phrases below. When you finish, the letters in the boxes will spell out a phrase.

1. grieving — mou[r]ning
2. recall — rem[e]mber
3. materials, machinery — equip[m]ent
4. stroked — patt[e]d
5. one who works the land — far[m]er
6. answers "why?" — [b]ecause
7. farmhouse — home[s]tead
8. needlework — stitche[r]y
9. finance record-keeper — account[a]nt
10. child learning to walk — todd[l]er
11. quietly — si[l]ently
12. fragile — f[r]ail
13. bird call — c[o]o
14. boy — [l]ad
15. unusual — frea[k]
16. gazing — [s]taring

Extension: Write to or talk with your grandparents about their lives. Write down some of their stories. Visit homes of elderly people you know.

Page 31

A Long Way Off

Name _____

Using data collected from the class, complete the graph below. You will need to write in the name of each star and graph its distance from our solar system.

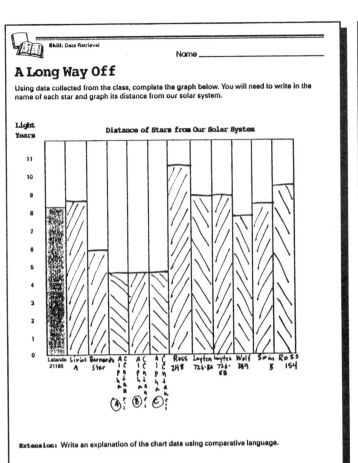

Distance of Stars from Our Solar System

Light Years

Extension: Write an explanation of the chart data using comparative language.

Page 33

Muddy–Muck–Muck

Name _____

Match the adjectives below to the boy(s) you think they best describe. Write each word in the appropriate circle. Be ready to defend your decision.

Word Bank				
friendly	compassionate	angry	puzzled	bullish
fearful	understanding	defensive	cowardly	horrified
kind	thoughtful	happy	wise	obstinate
offensive	selfish	helpful	rude	threatening

Answers may vary.

Tom

Bob

Wes

Sean

Henry

Extension: Act out one of these adjectives and have your classmates guess which one you have in mind.

Page 35

Scavenger Hunt

Name _____

Use the signs on the previous page to answer the following questions.

1. What was the speed limit? __30 mph__
2. What was the name of the ball park? __Kaline Ball Park__
3. What is "less filling?" __Dr. Nipsy__
4. What street did they find? __Terrace Boulevard__
5. What flavor of mayonnaise was advertised? __Avocado Mayo__
6. When was *The Music Man* showing? __August 11–15__
7. What was the radio station's slogan? __The station that puts you to sleep.__
8. What is "sehr gut?" __Tante's Strudelhaus__
9. What is Number 14? __Igloo school bus__
10. Who is Mary Tsoski? __She is running for school board__
11. What is the name of the Med Center? __Heimlich__
12. What is Englewood's proud title? __Sweat sock capital of the world__
13. What "ain't cheap?" __Penny loafers__
14. When should you honk? __if you love Elvis__
15. What is the fifth? __Federal Bank__
16. What is the last word on the Bunyan sign? __DROP__
17. How many signs are listed? __21__
18. How many signs have only four words? __6__

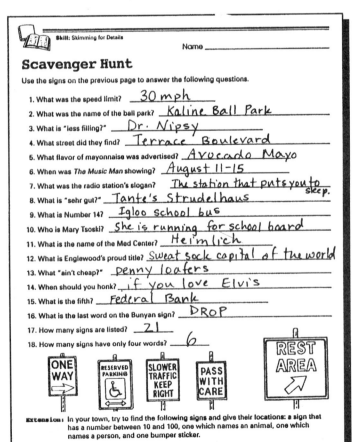

Extension: In your town, try to find the following signs and give their locations: a sign that has a number between 10 and 100, one which names an animal, one which names a person, and one bumper sticker.

Page 37

Snowball

Name _____

Answer these questions.

1. What kind of parent do you imagine Mrs. Wordsmith is? List three clues.
   __Answers may vary.__

2. *Snowball* is a simple name. What might be a more humorous name? . . . a more regal name? . . . a more prophetic name?
   __Answers will vary.__

3. What other games might a six-year-old boy play with his cat?
   __Answers will vary.__

4. How do you imagine the cat was injured? Explain.
   __Accept reasonable responses.__

5. Other than a pet's death, what events might cause a child to feel like Henry did at the end of *Snowball.*
   __Accept reasonable responses.__

6. How might Mrs. Wordsmith best help her son following the cat's death? Explain.
   __Accept reasonable responses.__

Extension: In one or two paragraphs describe either 1) a painful experience you had or 2) a painful experience you could have had.

Page 39
